Volume

Children's Word Games and Crossword Puzzles

For Ages 7 to 9

Edited by Eugene T. Maleska

TIMES
T
BOOKS

ISBN 0-812-91980-7

Laser typesetting by Ewing Systems, New York, New York
Manufactured in the United States of America

9 8 7 6 5 4 3

Introduction

Dear Girls and Boys,

It's so nice to know that you like the books that my friends and I have put together for you. How do I know that you're enjoying them? Well, because we have almost sold out the first two volumes and the publisher has asked us to prepare a third one.

So here's the book! We hope you have lots of fun and learn something at the same time.

One more thing. Whenever you get stuck, ask your parents or grandparents to give you a hint. We're sure they will be glad to help you here and there.

Sincerely,

E.T.M.

Familiar People
by Sam Lake

1

Across

1 Group of papers for writing notes
4 Person who flies a plane or steers a ship
6 Opposite of down
7 Another word for Dad or Pop
8 He picked a pack of pickled peppers
10 Cowboy Rogers

Down

1 What 8 Across was
2 Actor Pacino
3 Least brainy of the Seven Dwarfs
4 Young dog or seal
5 This is sometimes used for paving a road
9 "As I was going _____ St. Ives . . ."

Circle Fun
2
by Louis Sabin

✎ You can make a two–letter word by drawing a straight line between the O and a letter in the ring. We made eight two–letter words. Can you find all of them?

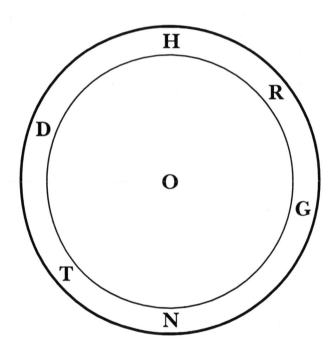

3 Climb Aboard
by June Boggs

✎ Using the definitions below, fill in the blanks of the ladder rungs.

Ladder Rungs

1 Something sweet

2 Opposite of subtracted

3 Melting snow

4 Dark time

5 Word before "Claus"

6 Shaped like a ball

7 Part of a flower

8 Cobra or python

Ladder Sides

1 What is on our flag

2 Flag colors

	1		2
1	S		R
2	A		D
3	S		H
4	N		T
5	S		A
6	R		D
7	P		L
8	S		E

3

4 What's in the School?
by Merryl Maleska Wilbur

To give you a start, the first letter of each word has been filled in.

1 It's red, white, and blue

2 You write with these

3 A through Z

4 Students sit at them

5 The teacher writes with this

6 They're filled with stories

7 They help you measure

8 You use these for mistakes

9 Part of an art class

10 It comes with or without lines

11 They help you cut

1 F ☐☐☐

2 P ☐☐☐☐☐☐

3 A ☐☐☐☐☐☐☐

4 D ☐☐☐☐

5 C ☐☐☐☐

6 B ☐☐☐☐

7 R ☐☐☐☐☐☐

8 E ☐☐☐☐☐☐☐

9 P ☐☐☐

10 P ☐☐☐☐

11 S ☐☐☐☐☐☐☐☐

5 My Schoolroom
by Rita M. Yelle

✏ In the puzzle below you will find sixteen things you usually see in your schoolroom. How many can you find?

```
B  L  O  A  F  D  C  L  O  C  K  G  S
C  L  R  L  T  E  U  A  M  R  O  G  T
G  P  A  I  D  S  M  C  H  A  L  K  N
T  G  O  C  Z  K  Y  X  N  U  N  S  E
A  E  R  M  K  S  G  H  E  O  R  S  D
S  P  L  A  N  B  T  I  L  E  E  P  U
P  C  K  E  M  K  O  B  S  A  T  M  T
E  P  I  S  V  U  W  A  Y  L  S  G  S
N  O  A  S  R  I  R  G  R  X  O  L  S
C  N  S  P  S  E  S  T  A  D  P  O  K
I  X  A  S  E  O  C  I  B  K  L  B  O
L  M  O  O  K  R  R  M  O  N  G  E  O
S  Y  K  M  L  P  S  S  S  N  T  R  B
```

1	Blackboard	9	Globe
2	Erasers	10	Map
3	Clock	11	Books
4	Desks	12	Students
5	Pencils	13	Poster
6	Chalk	14	Flag
7	Television	15	Scissors
8	Papers	16	Glue

6 Picture Puzzle
by Louis Sabin

✎ Hint: You have to open your hand to get rid of it.

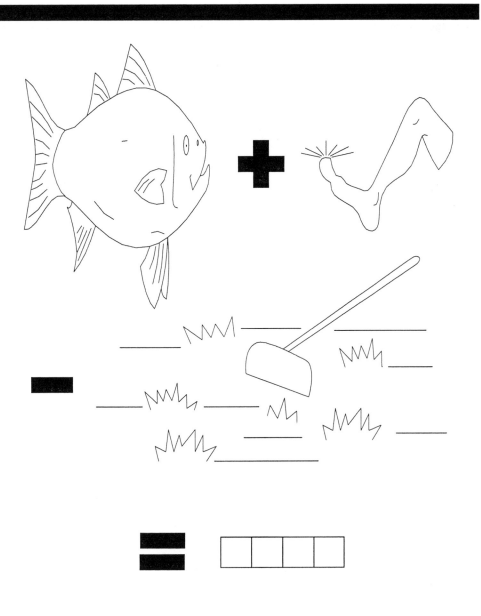

7 Alphabet Soup

by Merryl Maleska Wilbur

✎ Look at the clues below. Then fill in the boxes on the opposite page.

A   "Ready, _____, fire!"

B   Its baby is a cub

C   A grown-up kitten

D   A plate or a bowl

E   Finish

F   Part of a fish

G   Door in a fence

H   A kiss and a _____

I   Poison _____ makes you itch

J   Jelly comes in this

K   Where your leg bends

L   Opposite of high

M   It's used to wash a floor

N   It's used to catch butterflies

O   Place to bake fish or pizzas

P   You write with this

Q   Short test

R   Color of an apple

S   Opposite of happy

T   Nine plus one

U   "Once _____ a time"

V   Promise made by bride or groom

W   Dogs' tails do this

X   It shows broken bones

Y   Opposite of older

Z   Number before one

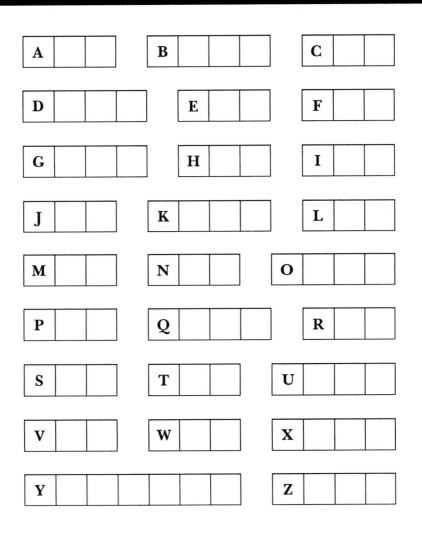

8 Birds and Fish
by Sam Lake

✎ Here's a mixture of creatures with wings and fins. To give you a start, we have placed a FLOUNDER in the right spot. Now try to fill in the others listed below.

DUCK

EAGLE

EEL

GEESE

RAVEN

SEAGULL

SHARK

SPARROW

TURKEY

VULTURE

|F|L|O|U|N|D|E|R|

Words That Sound Alike
by Walter Covell

9

Fill the blanks in the verses with the words shown in the eight sets.

FEAT	HERE	MEAT	MALE	PALE	PEEK	REIGN	TIDE
FEET	HEAR	MEET	MAIL	PAIL	PEAK	RAIN	TIED

1
A butcher is the one she'll _____
When Mom is shopping to buy _____.

2
Your letter carrier might be _____,
But women, too, deliver _____!

3
To distance runners it's a _____
To win a race without tired _____.

4
Was Jill upset and turning _____
When Jack fell down, dropping the _____?

5
If TV sound is hard to _____,
Just raise the volume . . . this dial _____!

6
A king or queen is known to _____
As well in sunshine as in _____.

7
Look! On the beach a boat is _____,
It won't be carried by the _____!

8
On an airplane take a _____;
You may spy a mountain _____.

11

10 Add a Letter
by Louis Sabin

✎ By adding a letter to every second and third word, you get a new word.

EXAMPLE:

"See a _____ and pick it up"		P	I	N
Whirl, like a top	S	P	I	N
Backbone	S	P	I	N	E

NOW TRY THESE:

Group 1

Use an oar ___ ___ ___

Black bird ___ ___ ___ ___

A king wears one ___ ___ ___ ___ ___

Group 2

"Thanks a _____ !" ___ ___ ___

Opening for a coin ___ ___ ___ ___

Slow-moving animal ___ ___ ___ ___ ___

Group 3

Sprint; dash ___ ___ ___

Smallest pup in a litter ___ ___ ___ ___

Grumble; hog's sound ___ ___ ___ ___ ___

11 Antonyms
by Rita M. Yelle

Antonyms are words that have opposite meanings. Find the word in the second column that is the exact opposite of the word in the first column. Then write it in the middle.

1	High	_____	Thin
2	Top	_____	Smooth
3	Big	_____	Low
4	Black	_____	Hard
5	Short	_____	Bottom
6	Fast	_____	Sour
7	Dark	_____	Small
8	Noisy	_____	Cold
9	Fat	_____	White
10	Wide	_____	Light
11	Rough	_____	Tall
12	Sweet	_____	Slow
13	Hot	_____	Quiet
14	Winter	_____	Narrow
15	Soft	_____	Summer

12 Green Things
by June Boggs

 Fill in the blanks.

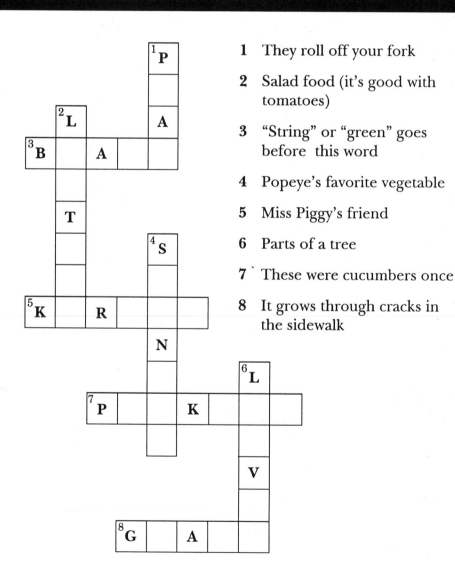

1   They roll off your fork

2   Salad food (it's good with tomatoes)

3   "String" or "green" goes before this word

4   Popeye's favorite vegetable

5   Miss Piggy's friend

6   Parts of a tree

7   These were cucumbers once

8   It grows through cracks in the sidewalk

Mix 'n' Match
by Merryl Maleska Wilbur

✏ Each animal below is missing some part or parts.
Draw lines to connect the animals with the missing parts.

1   **A**   Tail

2   **B**   Teeth

3   **C**   Whiskers

4   **D**   Tusks and trunk

5   **E**   Beak

✏ Now, spell the names of the five animals.

1 __ __ __ __ __ __ __ __

2 __ __ __ __ __

3 __ __ __ __

4 __ __ __ __ __ __ __ __ __

5 __ __ __

14 Wild and Tame Animals

by Sam Lake

Across

1 What animals lost their mittens?

3 This animal has horns and is related to a sheep

5 What kind of animal is Bambi?

6 She lives on a dairy farm and gives us milk

8 His first name could be Peter or Roger, and he is often called a bunny

12 This wild animal lives in Africa, but sometimes you can see him in a circus where a tamer makes him do tricks

Down

2 This fierce animal lives in India and has stripes and orange fur

4 Some children like to cuddle up in bed with a teddy _____.

6 What kind of animal is Garfield?

7 What animal is in the story of Little Red Riding Hood?

9 A gorilla is sometimes called an _____

10 He is the father of a calf

11 When this animal is born, he is called a puppy

15 Fairy-Tale Words
by Louis Sabin

Across

1 "Are you coming _____ going?"
3 "_____ Grandma's house I go!"
5 Word for a witch
7 "Tom, Tom the Piper's _____"
8 Smiling dwarf in *Snow White*
10 Foot part
11 Not-so-smart dwarf in *Snow White*
13 Opposite of against
14 "Daniel in the Lion's _____"
16 Goldilocks sat _____ the table
17 Rapunzel's hair was _____ long!

Down

1 "_____ boy!"
2 Fan's cheer
3 Something you get for Christmas
4 The prince sat _____ his horse
6 Creature like a croc
7 Go fast, like Roadrunner
9 Some people like _____ music
11 _____ your i's and cross your t's
12 "_____ sir, three bags full"
13 Do, re, mi, _____, sol . . .
15 "Jack Sprat could eat _____ fat"

16 The Famous Turtles Need Help

by June Boggs

 Please fill in the words for them.

1 Spinning toy
2 It burns and has flames
3 Our planet
4 Log house
5 Person in a play
6 Insect
7 Six plus five
8 Sweep with this
9 Western state
10 It's below your ankle
11 Not asleep
12 Lady who wears a crown
13 Very little
14 Farm building
15 Frozen water
16 Circus person who is funny
17 Faraway land near China
18 Yellow fruit that grows in bunches
19 Study for this
20 "Happy Birthday to _____"
21 Large stream
22 Ernie's friend
23 Ha-ha
24 President Bush's first name
25 Afraid

Thank you!

21

Name the Baby
by Rita M. Yelle

Do you know what we call a baby animal or bird? Below is a list of them and their babies. See if you can match them up correctly.

1	Cat	_____	Piglet
2	Dog	_____	Duckling
3	Bear	_____	Kitten
4	Deer	_____	Chick
5	Cow	_____	Puppy
6	Horse	_____	Joey
7	Sheep	_____	Cub
8	Hen	_____	Calf
9	Kangaroo	_____	Fawn
10	Duck	_____	Colt
11	Pig	_____	Lamb

18 Ant Farm
by Louis Sabin

✎ Here are ten words that have ANT in them. Can you get all ten?

1 I _____ to go home

2 A newborn baby is an _____

3 The largest land animal is an _____

4 A bush, a tree, or a shrub is a _____

5 A very big person, like Goliath, is a _____

6 Ulysses S. _____ was a U.S. President

7 He put on his _____ one leg at a time

8 A well-known Christmas visitor is called _____

9 A miner's lamp is called a _____

10 Donatello is a Teenage _____ Ninja Turtle

19 Do You Know Your XYZ's?

by June Boggs

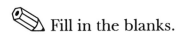 Fill in the blanks.

1   Candle __ __ x

2   Boston Red __ __ x

3   Jack-in-the-__ __ x

4   Can you __ __ x the broken toy?

5   __ __ x __ __ is a large state.

6   I love y __ __.

7   Bugs __ __ __ __ y

8   Fourth of __ __ __ y

9   Peanut butter and __ __ __ __ y

10   Can you __ __ __ y the piano?

11   One minus one is z __ __ __.

12   What __ __ z __ are your shoes?

13   The striped animal is a z __ __ __ __.

14   The z __ __ __ __ __ on my jacket is stuck.

15   He won first __ __ __ z __ in the race.

Across

1 The game called Tic _____ Toe has X's and O's
4 This is sweet and is used by people who make candy
6 An indoor building used for sports is called an _____
7 What are Lawrence Taylor's initials?
8 If somebody tags you, then you're _____
9 When nobody else is in the house, you're all _____
11 This word means *prevent*
12 How do you abbreviate *saints* or *streets*?

Down

1 Donatello and Michaelangelo are two of the Ninja _____
2 If you're almost ten years old, your _____ is nine
3 Dogs or some of your teeth are called _____
4 Potato _____ is a popular dish in the summertime
5 A person who marks test papers is a _____
10 Mel _____ was a famous baseball player

25

21 Fun and Games
by Walter Covell

Across

5   A game like tennis, played on a table with paddles

7   A game played on a board having kings, queens, bishops, knights, rooks, and pawns

9   A game played on the sidewalk

Down

1   Pictures made when you fit together small pieces made of wood or cardboard

2   A chasing game in which the one who is touched is "it"

3   A game in which you throw at a target

4   A game on a table with six pockets

6   A game played on a board having red and black squares

8   A game in which you must match dotted numbers

22 Friends in Hiding
by Walter Covell

✎ The name each friend listed below is hidden in a new word when a letter is written in the blank. The clue beside each name shows what the new word means.

1	__ A L F	A baby cow
2	A __ M Y	A lot of soldiers
3	__ A R T	Something to ride in
4	B E A __	A furry animal
5	B E E __	A red vegetable
6	B E __ N	A green vegetable
7	F L O __	Move like water in a river
8	G U S __	A puff of wind
9	H A __ L	Frozen rain
10	K I T __	It flies on a string
11	L E __ N	What Mrs. Sprat couldn't eat
12	M A __ T	It holds a sail
13	P A __ M	A coconut tree
14	P A T __	A narrow walkway
15	R O B __	Something to wear
16	R O __ D	Be careful crossing it
17	__ R O N	Press clothes
18	S __ A M	There's one on a baseball
19	S __ I D	Rode on a sled
20	T __ E D	Made a knot

28

23 Word Chain
by Merryl Maleska Wilbur

In this puzzle the last letter of one word is the first letter of the next. Use the clues to fill in words. Then, when you have finished the puzzle, write each numbered letter on the matching numbered blank to answer the riddle.

𝕽𝖎𝖉𝖉𝖑𝖊 𝕼𝖚𝖊𝖘𝖙𝖎𝖔𝖓

What has a trunk but needs no key,
And has a bark but won't bite me?

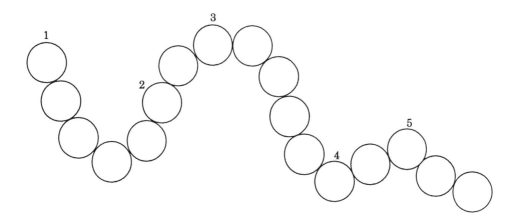

1 Someone who draws and paints
2 It's used to pave roads
3 Noise some snakes make; also, a baby's toy
4 You see with it
5 Have lunch

Riddle Answer: ___ ___ ___ ___ ___
                              1   2   3   4   5

24 Hear! Hear!
by June Boggs

✎ Here are some sounds we hear often. Write the name of whatever it is that makes each sound.

> It's noisy around here!

Moo	— — — —
Baa	— — — — —
Woof	— — — —
Hoot	— — — —
Meow	— — — —
Beep	— — — — —
Oink	— — — —
Buzz	— — — —
Hiss	— — — — —
Quack	— — — —
Cluck	— — — —
Tweet	— — — — —
Splash	— — — — —
Gobble	— — — — — —
Heehaw	— — — — — —
Achoo	— — — — — — —
Ticktock	— — — — —
Dingdong	— — — — —
Clippety-clop	— — — — — —
Cock-a-doodle-doo	— — — — — — —

25 The Children's Zoo
by Rita M. Yelle

✎ In the puzzle below you will find eighteen things that you might see in a children's zoo. How many can you find?

```
M  P  W  C  H  I  C  K  S  K  I  L  R
X  O  O  R  A  E  A  G  L  E  Q  A  O
Y  Z  N  L  W  N  W  A  F  O  B  D  R
N  E  M  K  K  R  F  N  G  B  S  M  P
O  K  T  I  E  F  D  C  I  M  P  U  S
P  A  L  T  X  Y  Z  T  P  M  P  S  E
O  N  A  T  R  M  S  F  G  P  H  O  S
D  S  L  E  C  N  E  S  I  X  L  R  E
L  W  S  N  K  C  G  E  S  P  O  G  E
O  N  W  S  I  R  S  U  O  K  M  F  G
C  R  G  M  S  O  P  A  K  S  C  H  O
B  A  B  Y  L  A  M  B  F  E  E  U  N
K  L  A  O  N  O  O  C  C  A  R  S  D
```

1	Monkeys	10	Mice
2	Chicks	11	Geese
3	Pony	12	Snake
4	Kittens	13	Fox
5	Pig	14	Hawk
6	Puppies	15	Raccoon
7	Ducks	16	Eagle
8	Baby lamb	17	Rabbits
9	Owl	18	Fawn

26 Some Heroes
by Carol Atkinson

✏ Clue: They go to blazes.

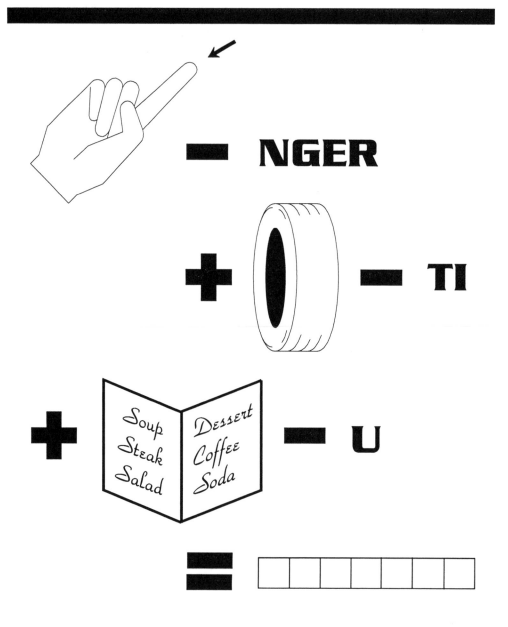

— **NGER**

+ ⭕ **—** **TI**

+ 📖 (Soup Steak Salad / Dessert Coffee Soda) **—** **U**

= ▢▢▢▢▢▢▢

27 To and Fro
by Walter Covell

✎ If written backward, the same letters that spell a word can spell another word. For example, FLOW and WOLF. The three-letter words below have the same letters forward and backward. Can you guess them?

Forward	Backward
1 Angry __ __ __ (Starts with M)	__ __ __ What a beaver builds
2 One of the Seven Dwarfs __ __ __ (Starts with D)	__ __ __ A fish
3 Something to chew __ __ __ (Starts with G)	__ __ __ Cup
4 Friend __ __ __ (Starts with P)	__ __ __ A place to sit
5 Short sleep __ __ __ (Starts with N)	__ __ __ Something to cook in
6 It divides a tennis court __ __ __ (Starts with N)	__ __ __ Number of your toes
7 Small bite __ __ __ (Starts with N)	__ __ __ Pointed fastener
8 Came in first __ __ __ (Starts with W)	__ __ __ At this time
9 Deep hole __ __ __ (Starts with P)	__ __ __ End of a pencil
10 This looks like a big mouse __ __ __ (Starts with R)	__ __ __ This covers roads sometimes

28 Computer Scramble
by Merryl Maleska Wilbur

✎ Matthew left his mother an important message on the computer screen. But the computer has a problem, and all the letters came out as numbers! On the lines below, write the letter that goes with each number to help Matthew's mom unscramble the message and to find out where he is.

4-5-1-18 13-15-13,
7-18-1-14-4-13-1 20-15-15-11 13-5
20-15 20-8-5 13-1-12-12 20-15
7-5-20 14-5-23 7-25-13 19-8-15-5-19.
23-5'12-12 2-5 8-15-13-5 6-15-18
4-9-14-14-5-18.

12-15-22-5,
13-1-20-20-8-5-23

A=1	B=2	C=3	D=4	E=5	F=6	G=7	H=8	I=9	J=10
K=11	L=12	M=13	N=14	O=15	P=16	Q=17	R=18
S=19	T=20	U=21	V=22	W=23	X=24	Y=25	Z=26

— — — —   — — —,

— — — — — — —   — — — —   — —

— —   — — —   — — — —   — —

— — —   — — —   — — —   — — — — — —.

— —'— —   — —   — — — —   — — —

— — — — — —.

— — — —,

— — — — — —

29 Breakfast Time
by Rita M. Yelle

✎ In the puzzle below you will see sixteen things you might notice in your kitchen at breakfast time. How many can you find?

```
B  L  E  N  D  E  R  C  R  A  E  S  P
R  T  T  A  R  G  T  D  T  B  T  T  A
B  O  E  A  L  M  P  O  U  S  R  O  S
R  A  L  A  O  L  P  R  A  T  E  V  U
E  M  B  X  Y  E  S  A  G  S  T  E  G
A  N  A  F  E  L  E  N  K  X  T  M  I
D  S  T  F  O  A  V  G  M  P  U  E  L
R  T  F  U  P  S  I  E  S  A  B  O  R
Y  O  S  R  L  O  N  J  A  T  J  P  P
C  P  R  E  A  L  K  U  P  S  L  L  M
Z  X  W  O  T  M  S  I  O  G  I  R  T
S  O  C  P  E  A  I  C  S  P  A  N  S
T  R  L  M  S  P  L  E  S  T  R  O  K
```

1	Coffee pot	**9**	Sink
2	Toaster	**10**	Pans
3	Orange juice	**11**	Plates
4	Blender	**12**	Jam
5	Bread	**13**	Knives
6	Table	**14**	Tea
7	Stove	**15**	Pots
8	Towels	**16**	Butter

30 Helping Billy
by Sam Lake

✎ Billy's room is a mess! Everything is scattered around. His parents have given him ten minutes to unscramble things. Can you help him? Hint: #1 becomes something to read.

COLLIN LEECH

1	K O B O	_____
2	V O G E L	_____
3	A I R O D	_____
4	A B T	_____
5	W A R T E S E	_____
6	B O L T O A L F	_____
7	T O A L B I A S	_____
8	D E L S	_____
9	B A L M S E R	_____
10	J A S M A P A	_____

31 The Labels Game
by June Boggs

 Fill in the tag for each group. Example:

hide and seek hopscotch tag Nintendo •— | G | A | M | E | S |

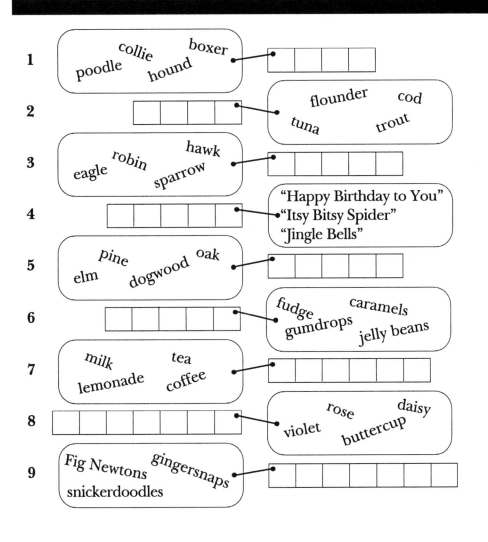

1 poodle collie hound boxer •—| | | | |

2 | | | | | —• flounder cod tuna trout

3 eagle robin hawk sparrow •—| | | | |

4 | | | | —• "Happy Birthday to You" "Itsy Bitsy Spider" "Jingle Bells"

5 elm pine dogwood oak •—| | | | |

6 | | | | —• fudge caramels gumdrops jelly beans

7 milk tea lemonade coffee •—| | | | | | |

8 | | | | | | —• rose daisy violet buttercup

9 Fig Newtons gingersnaps snickerdoodles •—| | | | | | |

In the Dark

32

by Merryl Maleska Wilbur

For each clue, write a word on the numbered puzzle pieces. Use the word box to help you find words. Then color in all the puzzle pieces with words that rhyme with *dark* to find a hidden animal.

1   Walk up a hill or go upstairs

2   A dog's sound

3   It tells time

4   Not odd

5   This minute; at this time

6   Place to sit on a bench or play ball

7   This can start a fire or be part of one

8   You use a pencil to make a _____

9   The number after seven

10   What you wash with

11   A bird with a pretty voice

12   They have toes

13   Relative of a rat

14   You sneeze when you have one

15   It meows

spark	eight	clock	climb	even	now	soap
cat	mark	bark	feet	mouse	lark	park	cold

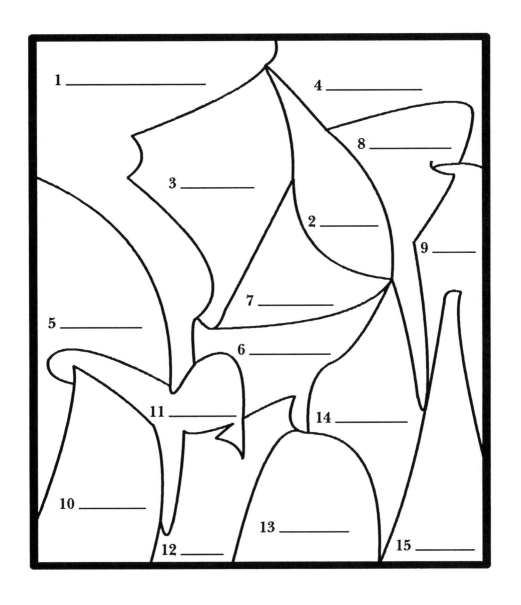

1 _____

4 _____

8 _____

3 _____

2 _____

9 _____

7 _____

5 _____

6 _____

11 _____

14 _____

10 _____

13 _____

12 _____

15 _____

Now you're no longer in the dark—

This animal is obviously a _____!

Find the Name
by Rita M. Yelle

✎ Look at line number one. You will see that one letter of the alphabet is used only once in the five words. When you spot that letter write it in the blank over number one at the bottom of the page. Do the same with the next nine lines.

When you have finished you will have spelled the name of a famous person.

1	DAME	WAND	MIND	SINS	SANE
2	POST	POET	STEP	SPAT	EGGS
3	COKE	ROSE	LAKE	ROME	CALM
4	CARE	WAKE	SICK	RACE	WISH
5	CODS	DIRT	ACTS	TROD	CAST
6	NOTE	RAPS	POLL	PARE	ROTS
7	GREW	BARS	DRAB	DARE	WEDS
8	DARN	TEND	PEAR	PEAL	LEAP
9	FAME	MITE	FOLK	KILT	TAME
10	WIRE	ROPE	POTS	SNOW	TILL

___ ___ ___ ___ ___ ___ ___ ___ ___ ___
 1   2   3   4   5   6   7   8   9 10

34 Numbers Game
by Walter Covell

✎ Can you fill the empty squares with the letters of the correct numbers from the list at the bottom of the page?

1 ☐☐☐☐☐ ripe tomatoes are hanging on a vine,

2 ☐☐☐ on another. That makes nine.

3 First, ☐☐☐☐ balls the player kicks.

4 Then, ☐☐☐ more. That totals six.

5 ☐☐☐☐ bears came out of their den.

6 As many from a second, altogether ☐☐☐!

7 ☐☐☐☐☐☐ tasty tarts were piled on a plate.

8 ☐☐☐☐☐☐ fell off, and left only eight.

TWO	TWO	FOUR	FIVE
SEVEN	TEN	TWELVE	TWENTY

41

Fill In the Blanks
by Sam Lake

	1	2	3	4	5	
6						7
8			■	9		
10			11			
■	12					■

Across

1 A square has four _____

6 Your mother and father are your _____

8 Pie _____ mode is pie with ice cream

9 "_____ many cooks spoil the soup"

10 The postman brings _____ to your house

12 "Have a _____ Christmas!"

Down

1 A town called _____ once had some witches

2 When you're very angry, you are _____

3 The letters between C and F are _____

4 The opposite of *to exit* is to _____

5 "The Three Little Pigs" is a _____ that little children like

6 If someone is your friend, you might say he's your _____

7 The letters _____ are used to call for help when a ship is sinking

11 President Teddy Roosevelt's initials were _____

Sentence Sense
by Merryl Maleska Wilbur

In the space next to or below the word box, or on a separate piece of paper, list all the words in the boxes with the number 1. Then do the same thing for the words in the boxes numbered 2, 3, 4, 5, and 6. Finally, write each list of words as a sentence to find out what Susannah and Vanessa had to do to get ready for their camping trip.

6 can	5 directions.	3 Have	4 Fill	2 out	6 Mom
3 air	1 sun	5 Mr.	3 bike	6 early	1 Buy
3 checked.	5 for	4 canteen	6 Wake	2 bags.	4 with
1 and	2 flashlight	6 so	1 spray.	3 tires	6 up
6 drive	5 Winfield	3 in	5 Call	1 bug	2 sleeping
2 and	1 block	6 us!	6 she	2 Get	4 water.

1 _____

2 _____

3 _____

4 _____

5 _____

6 _____

Answers

1

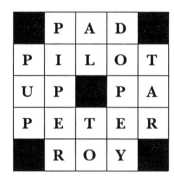

2

DO, GO, HO, NO, OH, ON, OR, TO

3

S	U	G	A	R
T				E
A	D	D	E	D
R				W
S	L	U	S	H
A				I
N	I	G	H	T
D				E
S	A	N	T	A
T				N
R	O	U	N	D
I				B
P	E	T	A	L
E				U
S	N	A	K	E

4

FLAG

PENCILS

ALPHABET

DESKS CHALK

BOOKS RULERS

ERASERS PAINT

PAPER SCISSORS

5

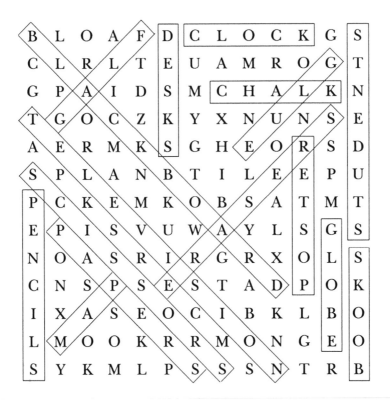

6

Fish + Toe - Hoe = Fist

7

| A | I | M |

| B | E | A | R |

| C | A | T |

| D | I | S | H |

| E | N | D |

| F | I | N |

| G | A | T | E |

| H | U | G |

| I | V | Y |

| J | A | R |

| K | N | E | E |

| L | O | W |

| M | O | P |

| N | E | T |

| O | V | E | N |

| P | E | N |

| Q | U | I | Z |

| R | E | D |

| S | A | D |

| T | E | N |

| U | P | O | N |

| V | O | W |

| W | A | G |

| X | R | A | Y |

| Y | O | U | N | G | E | R |

| Z | E | R | O |

8

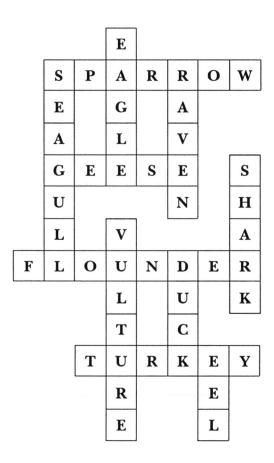

Answer to *Words That Sound Alike*

9

1.	Meet	**2.**	Male	**3.**	Feat	**4.**	Pale
	Meat		Mail		Feet		Pail
5.	Hear	**6.**	Reign	**7.**	Tied	**8.**	Peek
	Here		Rain		Tide		Peak

Answer to *Add a Letter*

10

1.	Row	**2.**	Lot	**3.**	Run
	Crow		Slot		Runt
	Crown		Sloth		Grunt

Answer to *Antonyms*

11

1. High–low
2. Top–bottom
3. Big–small
4. Black–white
5. Short–tall
6. Fast–slow
7. Dark–light
8. Noisy–quiet
9. Fat–thin
10. Wide–narrow
11. Rough–smooth
12. Sweet–sour
13. Hot–cold
14. Winter–summer
15. Soft–hard

12

1. Peas	**3.** Beans	**5.** Kermit	**7.** Pickles
2. Lettuce	**4.** Spinach	**6.** Leaves	**8.** Grass

Answer to *Mix 'n' Match*

13

1. D   **2.** A   **3.** E   **4.** B   **5.** C

1. Elephant
2. Tiger
3. Bird
4. Alligator
5. Cat

14

```
K I T T E N S
    I
    G O A T
  B E
D E E R      C O W
  A          A   O
  R A B B I T     L
  P     B     F
  E     U
        L   D
        L I O N
            G
```

15

```
O R       T O
H A G   S O N
  H A P P Y
  T O E
  D O P E Y
F O R   D E N
A T     S O
```

16

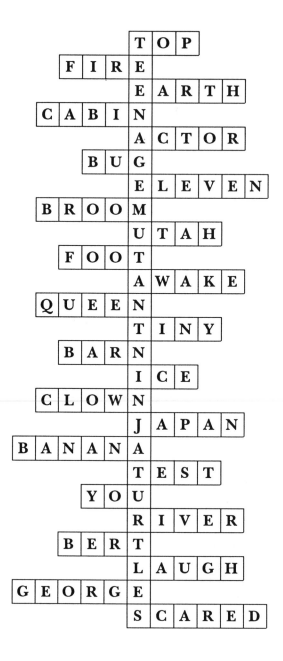

17

1. Cat–kitten
2. Dog–puppy
3. Bear–cub
4. Deer–fawn
5. Cow–calf
6. Horse–colt
7. Sheep–lamb
8. Hen–chick
9. Kangaroo–joey
10. Duck–duckling
11. Pig–piglet

18

1. Want
2. Infant
3. Elephant
4. Plant
5. Giant
6. Grant
7. Pants
8. Santa
9. Lantern
10. Mutant

19

1. Wax	**4.** Fix	**7.** Bunny	**10.** Play	**13.** Zebra
2. Sox	**5.** Texas	**8.** July	**11.** Zero	**14.** Zipper
3. Box	**6.** You	**9.** Jelly	**12.** Size	**15.** Prize

20

	T	A	C	
S	U	G	A	R
A	R	E	N	A
L	T		I	T
A	L	O	N	E
D	E	T	E	R
	S	T	S	

21

22

1.	CALF	6.	BEAN	11.	LEAN	16.	ROAD
2.	ARMY	7.	FLOW	12.	MAST	17.	IRON
3.	CART	8.	GUST	13.	PALM	18.	SEAM
4.	BEAR	9.	HAIL	14.	PATH	19.	SLID
5.	BEET	10.	KITE	15.	ROBE	20.	TIED

23

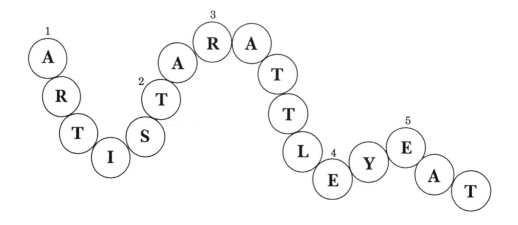

Riddle Answer: <u>A</u> <u>T</u> <u>R</u> <u>E</u> <u>E</u>
1 2 3 4 5

24

Moo	cow
Baa	sheep
Woof	dog
Hoot	owl
Meow	cat
Beep	horn
Oink	pig
Buzz	bee
Hiss	snake
Quack	duck
Cluck	hen
Tweet	bird
Splash	water
Gobble	turkey
Heehaw	donkey
Achoo	sneeze
Ticktock	clock
Dingdong	bell
Clippety-clop	horse
Cock-a-doodle-doo	rooster

25

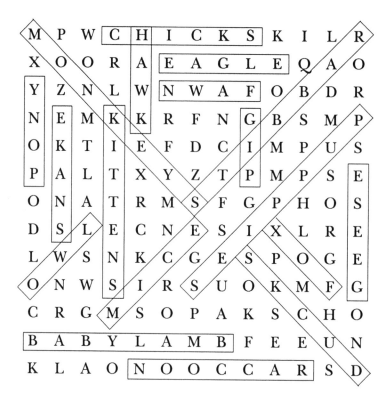

26

Finger - nger + Tire - Ti + Menu - u = Fireman

Answer to *To and Fro*

27

1.	MAD	/	DAM	**6.** NET	/	TEN
2.	DOC	/	COD	**7.** NIP	/	PIN
3.	GUM	/	MUG	**8.** WON	/	NOW
4.	PAL	/	LAP	**9.** PIT	/	TIP
5.	NAP	/	PAN	**10.** RAT	/	TAR

Answer to *Computer Scramble*

28

DEAR MOM,
GRANDMA TOOK ME
TO THE MALL TO
GET NEW GYM SHOES.
WE'LL BE HOME FOR
DINNER.

LOVE,
MATTHEW

61

29

```
B L E N D E R C R A E S P
R T T A R G T D T B T T A
B O E A L M P O U S R O S
R A L A O L P R A T E V U
E M B X Y E S A G S T E G
A N A F E L E N K X T M I
D S T F O A V G M P U E L
R T F U P S I E S A B O R
Y O S R L O N J A T J P P
C P R E A L K U P S L L M
Z X W O T M S I O G I R T
S O C P E A I C S P A N S
T R L M S P L E S T R O K
```

30

1. Book
2. Glove
3. Radio
4. Bat
5. Sweater
6. Football
7. Sailboat
8. Sled
9. Marbles
10. Pajamas

31

1.	Dogs	4.	Songs	7.	Drinks
2.	Fish	5.	Trees	8.	Flowers
3.	Birds	6.	Candy	9.	Cookies

32

1.	Climb	6.	Park	11.	Lark
2.	Bark	7.	Spark	12.	Feet
3.	Clock	8.	Mark	13.	Mouse
4.	Even	9.	Eight	14.	Cold
5.	Now	10.	Soap	15.	Cat

The animal is a **SHARK**.

33

WASHINGTON

34

1. Seven
2. Two
3. Four
4. Two

5. Five
6. Ten
7. Twenty
8. Twelve

35

	S	I	D	E	S	
P	A	R	E	N	T	S
A	L	A		T	O	O
L	E	T	T	E	R	S
	M	E	R	R	Y	

36

1. Buy sun block and bug spray.
2. Get out flashlight and sleeping bags.
3. Have air in bike tires checked.
4. Fill canteen with water
5. Call Mr. Winfield for directions.
6. Wake Mom up early so she can drive us!